Joanna MacGregor's PianoWorld

VERY FIRST ADVENTURES IN PIANO PLAYING

Saving the Piano
Book 1

MUSIC AND STORY BY JOANNA MACGREGOR
ILLUSTRATIONS BY STI

The optional *interactive CD* gives you the chance to go on a piano-playing with Ned, Grumper and the colourful PianoWorld cast. Listen to the whole story, use the black track numbers on each page to play along with the full performances and the accompaniments, and to take part in the musical games. Use the pause and repeat buttons on your CD player if you need more time or want to play a track several times.

The CD is a co-production between Faber Music Ltd and SoundCircus Ltd

Performers: Joanna MacGregor, Kathryn Oswald, Paul Ryan, Kieron Smith, Adam Stafford, Amanda Symonds / Script: Richard Williams / Producer: Nigel Wilkinson

For more information about PianoWorld and Joanna MacGregor, contact:
fabermusic.com/pianoworld and soundcircus.com

or Laura
© 2000 by Faber Music Ltd
First published in 2000 by Faber Music Ltd
Bloomsbury House
74–77 Great Russell Street
London WC1B 3DA
Original lyrics by Richard Williams
Cover design by Shireen Nathoo Design
Inside design by Geoffrey Wadsley
Music processed by Jeanne Fisher
Printed in England by Caligraving Ltd

ISBN10: 0-571-51671-8
EAN13: 978-0-571-51671-1

To buy Faber Music publications or to find out about the full range of titles available
please contact your local music retailer or Faber Music sales enquiries:

Faber Music Ltd, Burnt Mill, Elizabeth Way, Harlow CM20 2HX
Tel: +44 (0)1279 82 89 82   Fax: +44 (0)1279 82 89 83
sales@fabermusic.com   fabermusic.com

D1294487

FABER MUSIC

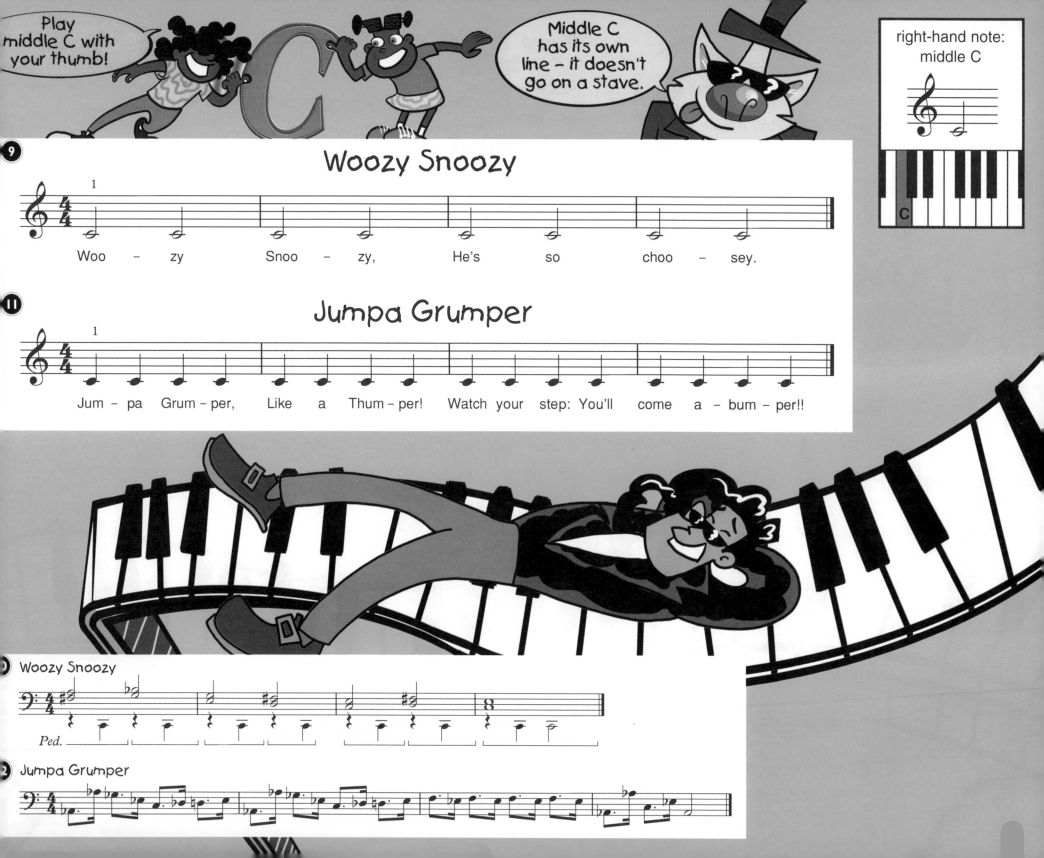

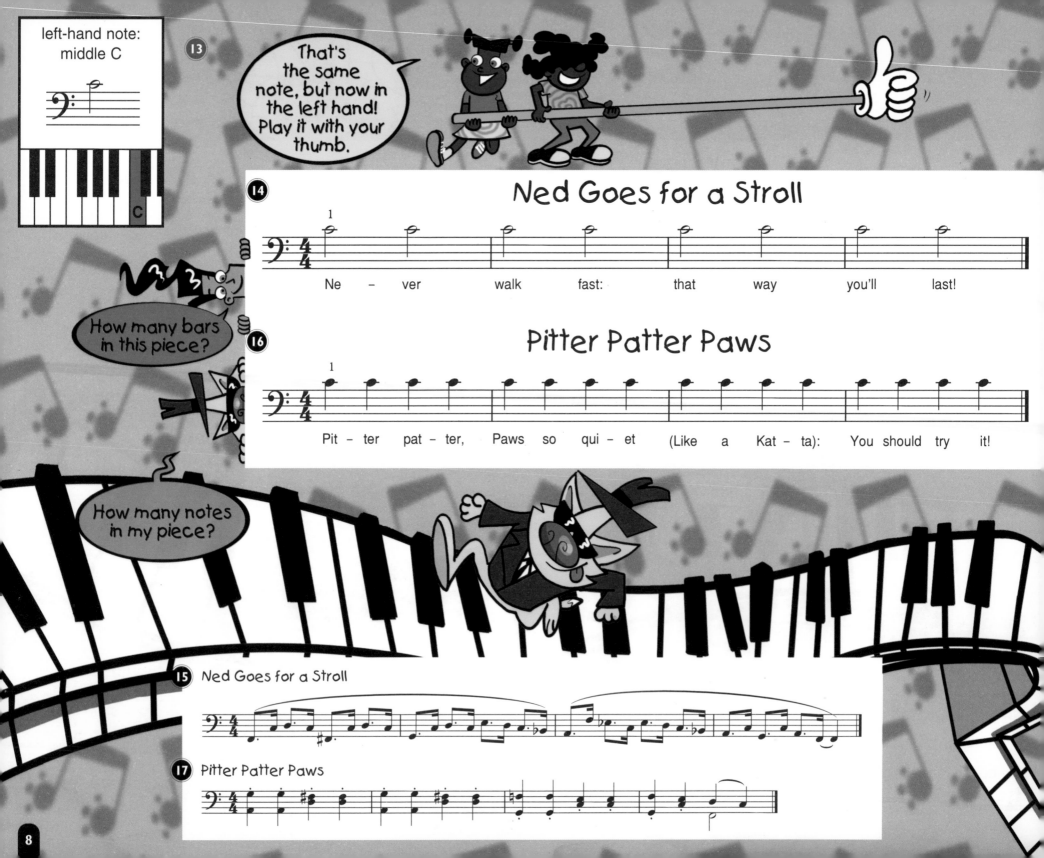

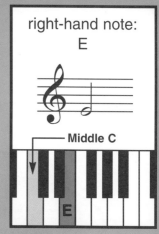

right-hand note:
E

Middle C

E

Digital Dodgems

37

38

Come on, Grumper!

f Come on, | lend a hand. | Play it loud – ly | like a band!

Come on Grum – per, | make it ring – | Scher – zo Sis – ters | want to sing!

Come on, Grumper!

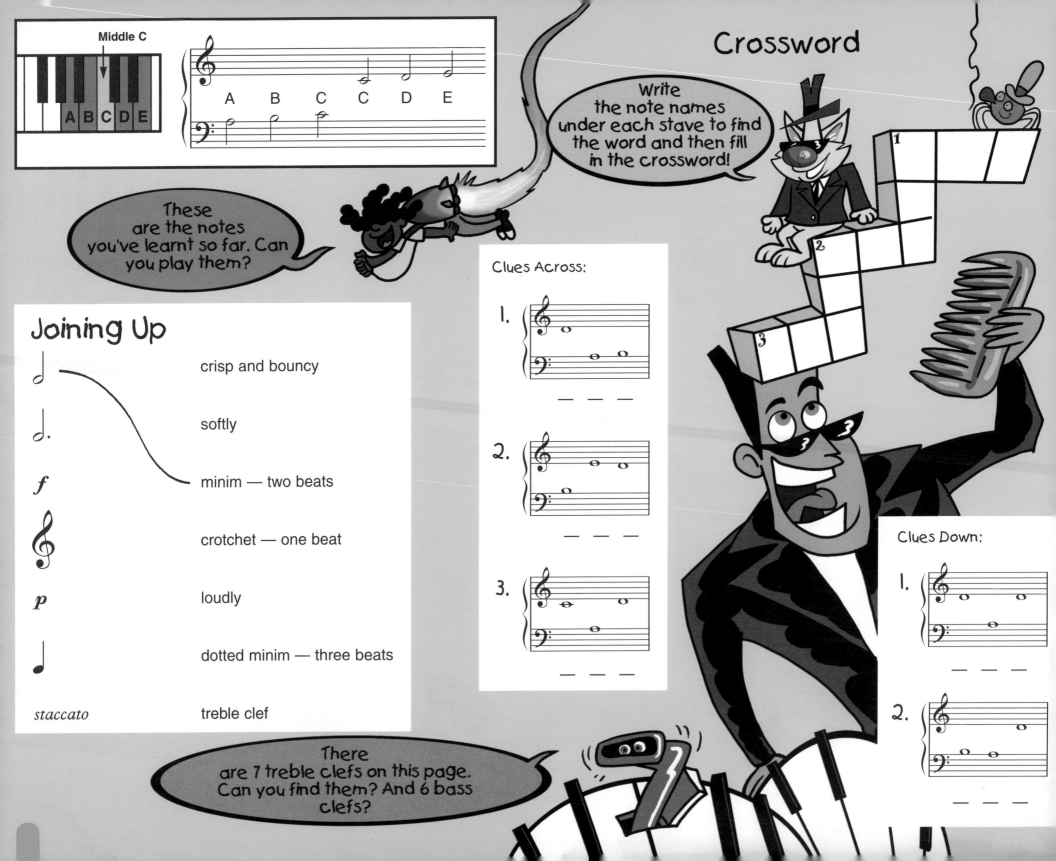

After that, you'll need a rest!

Rests are where there's a space in the tune.

Practise writing rests:

Crotchet rests

Minim rests

Fill in the Rests

Clap these rhythm duets with your teacher or a friend (or the CD), taking it in turns to do parts 1 and 2. Try playing the rhythms too (pick any note). Remember to count the beats of the bar out loud!

Clap and Play

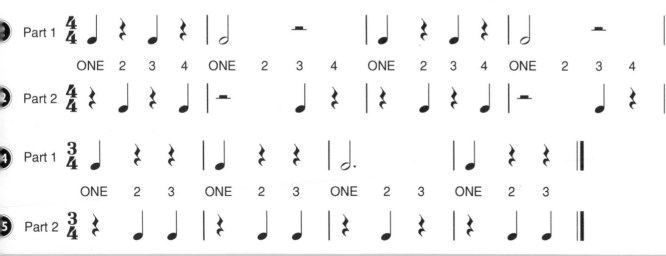

Part 1 — ONE 2 3 4 ONE 2 3 4 ONE 2 3 4 ONE 2 3 4

Part 2

Part 1 — ONE 2 3 ONE 2 3 ONE 2 3 ONE 2 3

Part 2

But one more thing – you may have guessed ...

17

♩♩ = 2 quavers = 1 ♩ beat.

The horizontal line joining the two quavers is called a 'beam'.

♪ = 1 quaver = ½ ♩ beat.

60 Clapping Games

Let us introduce you to the quaver
The crotchet lasts for one beat – but he's braver
Two quavers make a crotchet – what a raver!

Copy your teacher and clap these quaver rhythms.

ONE   and   2   and   ONE   and   2   and
2/4
Grum – per's Grunge,   Grum – per's Grunge.

ONE   and   2   and   ONE   and   2   and
2/4
Crash   Har – ry,   Crash   Har – ry.

ONE   and   2   and   3   and   ONE   and   2   and   3   and
3/4
Pit – ter   Pat – ter   Paws,   Pit – ter   Pat – ter   Paws.

Speeding Up!

61

Play this hands separately and then together.

1   2   3
4/4

1   2   3
Start   off   slow – – ly,   get – ting   speed   up,

go – ing   fast – er,   Now we're rush – ing, dash – ing, crash – ing,   STOP!

22

Learn G the other way round ...

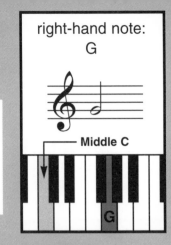

right-hand note:
G

Middle C

G

Digital Dodgems

Mmmmmm ...

Hot Cross Buns

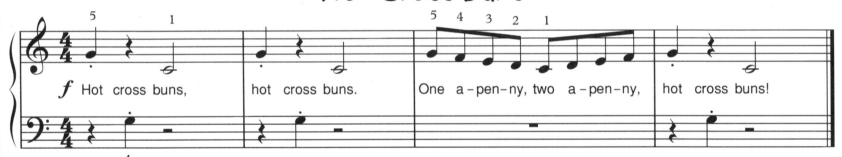

f Hot cross buns, | hot cross buns. | One a-pen-ny, two a-pen-ny, | hot cross buns!

Clap one part while your teacher claps the other – then swap round !

Don't Cook 'Em — Clap 'Em!

Part 1

Part 2

25

On this adventure, you've learnt all these notes.

Write the names of the notes in between the staves – and then play them.

Musical Sums

♩ + ♩ = __2__ beats   ♩ + ♩ = ___ beats

♩ + ♩ = ___ beats   ▬ + ♩ = ___ beats

♩ + 𝄽 = ___ beats   ♪ + ♪ + ♩ = ___ beats

Add these notes and rests together to work out the total numbers of beats.

Write the letter names under these notes to find out the words. I've done the first one.

Spell Check

F A C E   _ _ _ _ _   _ _ _ _ _ _

_ _ _ _ _   _ _ _ _ _   _ _ _ _

The Grand Old Duke of York

Hot Cross Bu
Don't Cook 'Em – Clap 'Em!
Jingling Bells
Jumpa Grumper
Woozy Snoozy (Without the music!)
Make up a tune in the left hand, using the notes you've learnt
The Grand Old Duke of York
Play the highest note on the piano, then the lowest note. Play 3 different tone clusters. Go back to 'Jingling Bells'
Play 'Come on, Grumper!' forwards. Then play it backwards.
Make up a rhythm and clap it
Ned's Dainty Dance
What To Do
Play any piece very softly
Give It Everything
FINISH

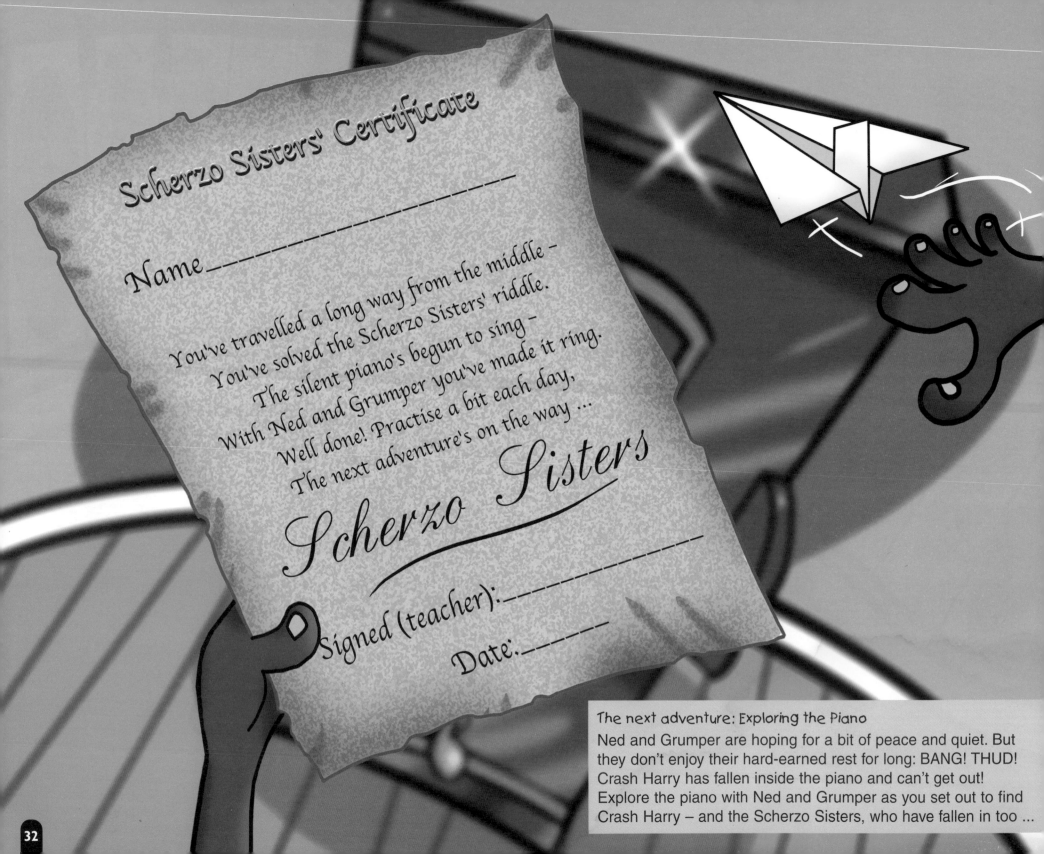

Scherzo Sisters' Certificate

Name_____

You've travelled a long way from the middle –
You've solved the Scherzo Sisters' riddle.
The silent piano's begun to sing –
With Ned and Grumper you've made it ring.
Well done! Practise a bit each day,
The next adventure's on the way ...

Scherzo Sisters
_____

Signed (teacher):_____

Date:_____

The next adventure: Exploring the Piano
Ned and Grumper are hoping for a bit of peace and quiet. But
they don't enjoy their hard-earned rest for long: BANG! THUD!
Crash Harry has fallen inside the piano and can't get out!
Explore the piano with Ned and Grumper as you set out to find
Crash Harry – and the Scherzo Sisters, who have fallen in too ...